W9-AMB-623

J.R.R. TOLKIEN

DAVID R. COLLINS

In Consultation with Martha Cosgrove,
M.A. and Reading Specialist

LERNER PUBLICATIONS COMPANY/MINNEAPOLIS

Martha Cosgrove has a master's degree from the University of Minnesota in secondary education, with an emphasis on developmental and remedial reading. She is licensed in 7–12 English and language arts, developmental reading, and remedial reading. She has had several works published, and she gives numerous state and national presentations in her areas of expertise.

Copyright © 2005 by David R. Collins

All rights reserved. International copyright secured. No part of this book may be reproduced, stored in a retrieval system, or transmitted in any form or by any means—electronic, mechanical, photocopying, recording, or otherwise—without the prior written permission of Lerner Publications Company, except for the inclusion of brief quotations in an acknowledged review.

Lerner Publications Company
A division of Lerner Publishing Group
241 First Avenue North
Minneapolis, Minnesota U.S.A.

Website address: www.lernerbooks.com

Library of Congress Cataloging-in-Publication Data

Collins, David R.
　　J. R. R. Tolkien / by David R. Collins.
　　　　p.　　cm. – (Just the facts biographies)
　　Includes bibliographical references and index.
　　ISBN: 0–8225–2470–8 (lib. bdg. : alk. paper)
　　1. Tolkien, J. R. R. (John Ronald Reuel), 1892–1973–Juvenile literature.
　2. Fantasy fiction, English–History and criticism–Juvenile literature.
　3. Authors, English–20th century–Biography–Juvenile literature.　4. Middle Earth (Imaginary place)–Juvenile literature.　I. Title.　II. Series.
　PR6039.032Z6225　2005
　828'.91209–dc22　　　　　　　　　　　　　　　　　　204005482

Manufactured in the United States of America
1　2　3　4　5　6　– JR – 10　09　08　07　06　05

CONTENTS

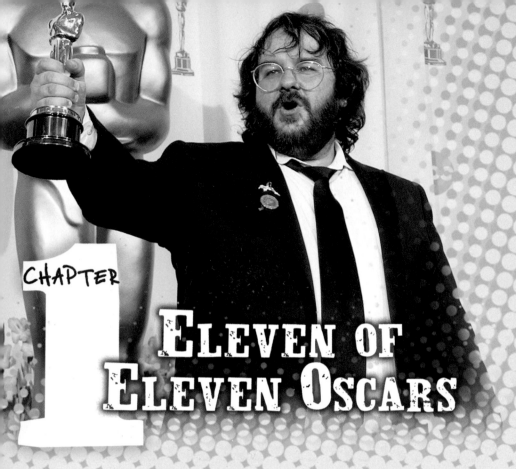

ELEVEN OF ELEVEN OSCARS

(Above)
Director Peter Jackson poses with one of the eleven Oscars received by *The Return of the King* **in 2004.**

WHAT IN THE WORLD would John Ronald Reuel Tolkien have thought about the hoopla and glitz of the 2004 Academy Awards? He was, after all, a professor of the English language who loved life in the quiet English countryside. He didn't think much of new machines and new technologies. He valued simple living and simple pleasures.

The Return of the King–the final film based on Tolkien's three-book fantasy epic *The Lord of*

4

the Rings, nicknamed LOTR–was honored with eleven Oscar nominations. Tolkien would probably have been uncomfortable with the public attention, with flashbulbs popping everywhere and members of the media chasing after actors for interviews. Even Peter Jackson, the director of the three LOTR movies, said "If only we could go and have a private dinner and award the Oscar at a restaurant with no TV cameras."

Professor Tolkien wouldn't have been much interested in the awards, even though this last movie won all eleven awards for which it was nominated. He might even have been a bit disappointed in some of the parts of his books that never made it to the screen. He likely would've been astounded at the billions of dollars the movies were making and all the fan websites that had popped up.

One thing he might've been glad to know was that some of those millions of moviegoers went back to read his original books. He'd spent more than ten years writing them and more years reworking them so they could be published. He'd created maps and a language that no one had ever seen or heard before. His writings had inspired artists to draw and moviemakers to dream large. Asked in an interview if he'd like to be remembered for his writings on the English language or for the LOTR trilogy, he said "I shouldn't have thought there was much choice in the matter–if I'm remembered at all it will be by *The Lord of the Rings*."

CHAPTER 2

TOLKIEN'S BEGINNINGS

A FULL MOON WAS IN THE SKY high above the grasslands of South Africa. Somewhere, a pack of wolves howled. A lone lion prowled, searching for prey. Snakes slithered in the moonlight.

Meanwhile, the people in the town of Bloemfontein slept. The town was a European community in a mostly black part of South Africa. Bloemfontein was a mix of old and new. It had stone-and-wood homes and churches, government buildings, a library, and a hospital. Small shops stood around the town square. But the wind swirled dust from the dirt streets. The city park was not very good, said one British resident named Mabel Tolkien.

Mabel and her husband, Arthur, were an attractive couple. They had both come to South Africa from Britain. People in town were used to seeing Mabel with her soft red hair pulled up in a popular style. The Tolkiens always seemed to be together. Some people said they always acted like newlyweds.

The birth of a son on January 3, 1892, added more joy to their lives. Mabel and Arthur gave the baby three names. His first name was John, after his grandfather. The second was Ronald, because both parents liked it. The third name was Reuel, Arthur's middle name. The parents usually just called the baby Ronald. But all his life, Ronald would enjoy writing all four of his initials, J. R. R. T.

IT'S A FACT!

The name Tolkien is of German origin. It translates as "foolishly brave" or "stupidly clever."

Arthur and Mabel rarely let Ronald out of their sight. The area they lived in was dangerous, and Ronald had several scary moments during his early years. For example, one afternoon while Ronald was sleeping, a neighbor's monkey got into his room. The animal chewed up some of the baby's clothes.

Months later, as Ronald learned to walk, he fell in the garden near a tarantula. The spider bit him. Ronald started crying and went to his nanny (the woman who helped care for him). She quickly sucked out the dangerous venom, or poison, from the bite. Her quick action saved Ronald, who did not suffer any bad effects from the bite.

IT'S A FACT!
Tolkien's early experience with the tarantula may have shaped the monster Shelob that appears in *The Lord of the Rings.*

These events scared Mabel. Monkeys and spiders—along with heat waves and swarms of insects—all made her dislike Bloemfontein. She kept thinking about going home to Britain, where she and Arthur had met.

THE TOLKIENS IN SOUTH AFRICA

When Mabel Suffield was seventeen, she met Arthur Tolkien in Birmingham, a city in the center of England. He was thirty and had a career in banking. Arthur had seen his father have money problems. He didn't want the same to happen to him. Arthur and Mabel dated, and shortly after her eighteenth birthday, they decided to get married. But Mabel's father said that he couldn't let his daughter marry so young. He made the couple wait. They shared their feelings in letters.

Arthur worked at Lloyds Bank in Birmingham. The job didn't pay well, and there was little hope of promotion. Meanwhile, the banking business in South Africa was very good, partly because gold and diamonds had been discovered there. At that time, South Africa was part of the huge British Empire. If they wanted to, British citizens could find work in other parts of the empire. Arthur found a job in South Africa and moved there. He hoped to find better job opportunities.

At first, Arthur traveled often on business. By the end of 1890, he was managing a branch of the Bank of Africa in Bloemfontein. The position paid well, and the bank gave him a house in the town. Arthur asked Mabel to join him as soon as she could.

She prepared to leave soon after her twenty-first birthday. In March 1891, she packed her trunks and boarded a ship that carried her toward South Africa. Three weeks later, Mabel landed in Cape Town, the South African capital. Arthur was there to greet her. The couple were married on April 16, 1891.

A busy street in Bloemfontein, South Africa

After a short honeymoon, the couple went to live in Bloemfontein. The 700-mile (1,120-kilometer) journey was like a trip into the past. The lifestyle was relaxed. The Tolkien home, next door to the bank, was open and comfortable.

As the wife of a bank manager, Mabel often entertained guests. At first, she enjoyed the social life, but she soon tired of it. Ronald's birth in 1892 made the couple very happy. But soon afterward, Arthur began traveling on

IT'S A FACT!

The name Bloemfontein in the South African language Afrikaans means "spring of flowers." The Sotho people of South Africa called the place Mangaung, meaning "place of the leopard."

business. In May, Mabel's sister visited. The visit reminded Mabel of how much she missed her family and friends in Britain.

On February 17, 1894, Mabel gave birth to another son, Hilary Arthur Reuel Tolkien. Mabel had to stop thinking of going back to Britain for a while. Hilary was a stronger child than Ronald. He quickly adjusted to the heat and dangers of Bloemfontein. But Ronald still suffered through the extremes of hot and cold weather. Mabel tried to find places to visit where conditions were better for him. When Ronald was three, his mother took the

Cape Town is near the ocean. It is cooler than Bloemfontein.

boys on a trip to Cape Town. There, they enjoyed the sandy beaches and fresh air.

One morning, shortly after returning to Bloemfontein, Ronald found his father with a paint-brush in his hand. Arthur had painted the letters A. R. TOLKIEN on the lid of a big trunk. He told Ronald that the trunk would soon be filled with clothes, ready for a trip. The three-year-old boy smiled. He would never forget that moment with his father.

THE LOSS OF A FATHER

In April 1895, Mabel Tolkien took her sons and their nanny on a boat to Britain. They expected Arthur to follow in a short time. They arrived in Birmingham within a month. Although Birmingham was an industrial city of smokestacks and factories, Mabel was happy to be home.

During the next few months, Ronald and Hilary met relatives they had never seen before. They lived with Mabel's parents, the Suffields. Grandfather Suffield, who had a long beard, liked to tell jokes. The old man loved playing with words. The young boys thought his word games were fun.

Arthur Tolkien remained in Bloemfontein. In his letters, he promised to come to Britain soon.

But months went by with no visit. At Christmas, Ronald and Hilary had their first large, decorated Christmas tree. They sang Christmas carols and ate special holiday food, such as Christmas pudding.

During this time, Mabel received news that Arthur was ill. She quickly arranged to take her sons back to Bloemfontein. Despite the fun he had been having, Ronald was excited to go home. He asked his nanny to write a letter from him to his father. In the letter, Ronald said that he was grown up and promised to show his father all of his Christmas presents.

Ronald's letter was never sent, and the boys never went back to South Africa. Arthur Tolkien died on February 15, 1896. He had rheumatic fever, a disease that can damage the heart. (Drugs to treat the disease didn't appear until the mid-1950s.) Ronald had just turned four. By the time his family learned of Arthur's death, he was already buried in a Bloemfontein graveyard 5,000 miles (8,000 km) away from Birmingham. Mabel was very sad and confused.

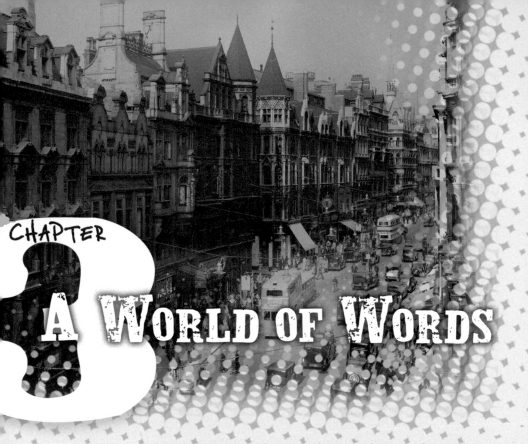

CHAPTER 3

A WORLD OF WORDS

RONALD AND HILARY enjoyed their life in Birmingham. Ronald had grown very fond of his grandfather. He often sat and watched as the old man drew a circle around a coin and then wrote long verses inside the circle. Ronald could print only a few letters inside the small space. Ronald also enjoyed his grandfather's tales of family history. Life was not all good, though. Arthur had not left the family much money, and Mabel needed more to raise her sons.

Mabel hoped that her sons would one day enter King Edward's School. It was

(Above) In the late 1800s, Birmingham, England, was a major center of manufacturing.

It's a Fact!

Many of the locations in *The Lord of the Rings* originated near Warwickshire, the old English county where Tolkien spent his childhood. He lived near Meon Hill, an ancient fort that was probably the inspiration for Weathertop. Ronald and Hilary explored Moseley Bog, a damp woodland near Sarehole Mill. The local miller often chased away the boys. The bog may have been the inspiration for the Old Forest. The grumpy miller may have become part of the character of Gandalf.

Birmingham's finest boys' school and the one their father had gone to. In the meantime, the family moved to a small brick house in Sarehole, a town near Birmingham in the county of Warwickshire. Ronald enjoyed the fresh air and the chance to explore the countryside.

Ronald thrived in the new setting and was soon able to read and write. Mabel taught him languages such as Latin and French. She tried to teach Ronald to play the piano, but he showed no interest. He was most interested in words. He enjoyed their sounds and shapes.

Ronald also liked to draw. He could sit happily

Tolkien's love for nature, especially trees, lasted his entire life.

for hours with a
pad and pencil.
Trees were one
of his favorite
subjects. Ronald
would first draw a tree, and then he would climb
the tree and talk to it. He thought of the trees as
friends. When a nearby weeping willow tree was
cut down, Ronald was sad for days.

Ronald also loved stories. He read some
stories on his own, while Mabel read others to
him. *Alice in Wonderland* by Lewis Carroll and
Andrew Lang's *The Red Fairy Book* were among his
favorites. He knew the stories well. When Mabel

read to Ronald, he wouldn't allow her to skip a single word. By the time he was seven, Ronald was writing his own stories. His first story, which he remembered even after he had grown up, was about a big green dragon.

A MOVE INTO THE CITY

In the fall of 1899, Ronald took the entrance tests for King Edward's School. He didn't pass the exams and had to wait another year to try again. If he got in, the school would charge money for him to attend. The next year, he passed. The school was 4 miles (6 km) from Sarehole. Mabel could not afford to send Ronald on the train to Birmingham every day, so the family moved into the city. Ronald hated to leave the trees and the countryside he loved and where he had been healthy and strong. He didn't like the family's new home nearly as much.

The Tolkiens also had some other big changes in their lives. Mabel had found strength in her Christian faith after Arthur's death. Like most English people, the family attended Anglican church services. But Mabel later decided to follow the Catholic faith, a different

King Edward's School in Birmingham prepared boys for higher education.

form of Christianity. Many members of her family didn't approve of the choice, but Mabel had made up her mind. She shared her new beliefs with her sons.

Soon it was time for Ronald to start at King Edward's. The school was a large building with high, carved walls and deep windows. It was covered with dirty black soot from smoking chimneys. Inside, the school echoed with the noise of students and the sound of nearby railway engines. Hundreds of students studied math, Latin, and other subjects on old wooden benches. It was a good school that helped many students get into England's best universities, especially Oxford and Cambridge.

John Ronald Reuel Tolkien got off to a slow start at the school. He was not used to noisy, crowded classrooms. He didn't like the competition with classmates for high grades. Ronald was used to his mother's teaching, and he struggled in his classes.

Soon after settling into their new home, the Tolkiens had to move again. Their house was going to be torn down to make room for a fire station. Ronald was happy to leave. Mabel found a larger house behind King's Heath Station. The back of the house faced a railroad line. It was also close to the home of Mabel's parents.

The new location opened up another world to Ronald. Behind the house, trains rumbled by, shaking everything. Engine whistles blew at all hours. Steam hissed from the engines. Trucks rolled

into a nearby coal yard. Ronald could hear the
sounds of people at work. Many of the coal trucks
had labels on their sides with words such as
Gwalia, Vavasour, and *Rhonabwy.* These were places
in Wales, which, like England, is part of Britain.
Wales was known for its many coal mines. Ronald
wondered what the Welsh words meant. He
couldn't even guess how to say them. But they
fascinated him.

Mabel continued to explore her religion. She
took her new Catholic faith very seriously. She
wanted her sons to get religious training at school.
She took Ronald out of King Edward's. Early in
1902, she entered her sons in St. Phillip's Catholic
School. Ronald was ten, and Hilary was eight.

RONALD'S EDUCATION

Ronald quickly became bored at St. Phillip's,
because he had already learned what his classmates
were studying. Mabel's decision to become a
Catholic had angered her family. They refused to
help her with money, so Mabel tutored her sons,
hoping they might get scholarships at King
Edward's. The scholarships would help to pay for
their schooling. Her work paid off. In the fall of

IT'S A FACT!

Founded by King Edward VI in 1552, King Edward's School for Boys is still going strong.

1903, Ronald was back at King Edward's. This time he wanted to stay.

Ronald was placed in the sixth class at King Edward's. It was a middle grade in a school that combined elementary school and high school. Ronald and his classmates studied ancient Greek, a language that Ronald immediately liked. It flowed smoothly, and he was fascinated by the ancient words. This fascination with words would stay with him all his life.

George Brewerton was one of Ronald's teachers. Brewerton was an interesting teacher because he did not just instruct. He performed, making every lesson a journey. He took the students into the past to show them the excitement and beauty of words. Brewerton demanded that his students listen well and think quickly. Ronald did both.

One morning, as Ronald sat on his bench, his teacher began another adventure. Brewerton began reading Geoffrey Chaucer's *The Canterbury Tales*.

Geoffrey Chaucer was more than a writer. He also worked for the English government as a diplomat and a tax collector.

Chaucer wrote the tales in the late 1300s. Many people consider *The Canterbury Tales* to be the best literary work in an old form of English called Middle English. Brewerton read aloud some verses in the old language.

Ronald listened carefully as Brewerton paused. He then repeated the same verses in modern English. Ronald was fascinated by the stories and enjoyed every word.

In *The Canterbury Tales,* Chaucer describes the lives of people from English society. Their words and actions tell about who they were. Chaucer's writing was frank and detailed. Brewerton wanted his students to write with similar freedom and openness. He told them to use plain words and to call a thing what it is rather than use a fancy description.

ABOUT ENGLISH

English is the world's most widely used language. It came from groups who lived in the area that later became Germany. Among these groups were the Angles and the Saxons. These tribes invaded England in the 400s—or more than 1,500 years ago. (In fact, the name England comes from Angle-land.)

The language the Angles and the Saxons spoke sounded more like modern German than like the English we know. Scholars call this version of English Old English. It was spoken throughout England until about 1066.

In 1066, England was again invaded. This time, the invaders were from what would become northern France. They were French-speaking Normans. The people of England borrowed a lot of French words and put them into English. The new, French-influenced language was called Middle English. It was widely used from the 1100s to the late 1400s, or until about 500 years ago.

Modern English dates from after the 1400s. Dialects (or local varieties) developed, including the kind of English spoken in the United States, in Australia, and in New Zealand. Tolkien enjoyed studying the origins of English and could read Old English and Middle English.

A page from an illustrated version of *The Canterbury Tales*

At Christmas in 1903, Mabel wrote to relatives and told them of Ronald's progress at school. She wrote that he knew more Greek than she knew Latin. She also bragged about his taking First Communion at church, an important step for a Catholic child. She wanted her family to be proud of her son's success.

FAMILY ILLNESSES

Early in 1904, the Tolkien family became ill with measles and whooping cough. These are two dangerous diseases that children often got. Mabel worked hard to nurse her sons back to health. But the work left her weak. By April, she was in the hospital. The doctor told her that she had diabetes. He told her to take a long rest. (Insulin treatment, which helps modern diabetics, was not available yet.)

A family friend and Catholic priest named Father Francis Morgan found the Tolkiens rooms in Woodside Cottage. The home was on land that belonged to a Catholic group, called the Oratory clergy. The local postman and his wife lived in the rest of Woodside Cottage. Mabel rested and fought to regain her health. During the summer, Ronald and Hilary enjoyed being outdoors. They explored the woods, climbed trees, and raced along paths and hillsides.

Ronald returned to King Edward's in the fall. Each morning, he got up while it was still dark. He walked a mile to the train station, then rode into Birmingham. Hilary remained at home. He met his older brother with a lantern when Ronald returned after school, again in the dark.

Mabel Tolkien's health grew worse that fall. In early November, she collapsed on the kitchen floor.

She remained unconscious for six days. On
November 14, 1904, she died. At the age of twelve,
John Ronald Reuel Tolkien was an orphan. He stood
with Hilary at their mother's bedside. The boys
looked sadly at the woman who lay before them.
The two boys must have felt empty and alone.

CHAPTER 4

EXCITING DISCOVERIES

FATHER FRANCIS MORGAN knew there was little time for grief. He also knew why Mabel had named him the guardian, or the decision maker, for her two sons. Mabel wanted Ronald and Hilary to be raised in the Catholic faith. Most of the boys' family would have refused to raise the boys as Catholics. But Beatrice Suffield, Mabel's sister-in-law and Ronald's aunt, had no strong religious feelings. She also had a room available in her home. Father Morgan quickly arranged for Ronald and Hilary to live with their aunt.

The boys paid little attention to Aunt Bea, and she paid little attention to her nephews. Father Morgan had asked her to feed and house the boys, and that is what she did. She was poor and had recently lost her husband, Mabel's brother. She showed little affection for her nephews.

Hilary adjusted quickly to the new surroundings, but Ronald missed the warm feelings of the past. Often he stood at the window of the top-floor bedroom and looked at all the rooftops outside. He could rarely see much of the countryside. Ronald felt like he was in prison. Hilary passed the time by throwing stones at cats in the street below.

Father Morgan kept a close watch over the boys. He made sure they were well fed and had good clothes. Mabel had left little money for her sons. Father Morgan often used his own money to pay for their things. Each morning, Ronald and Hilary left their room and put on altar-boy robes. They helped Father Morgan during Mass, the Catholic church service. After a quick breakfast, they went to school at King Edward's. If they were early, the boys walked. If they were running late, they took a streetcar pulled by horses.

IT'S A FACT!

Around the corner from Tolkien's aunt's house were two tall, fancy towers. They are said to be the inspiration behind Minas Morgul and Minas Tirith. These two towers represented cities in Tolkien's kingdom of Gondor.

STUDYING WORDS

In 1905, Ronald met Christopher Wiseman, the son of a Methodist minister. Methodism is yet another form of Christianity. Wiseman challenged Ronald in the classroom as well as in sports, such as rugby, a popular field game. From the moment they met, the two boys were constant companions. They talked about Latin and Greek for hours. They also enjoyed arguing about religion. They helped each other learn to look at difficult issues and to think in an organized way.

IT'S A FACT!

Rugby was invented in Britain in the 1800s. It is played all over the world. Each of the two opposing rugby teams tries to make points by kicking, passing, or carrying the oval ball to the opponents' goal line. Rugby has a lot in common with American football.

Latin and Greek were the main subjects of study at King Edward's. Ronald's classmates often struggled with the languages. They couldn't remember what words meant and couldn't pronounce them correctly. But Ronald loved the languages. He was excited for each new lesson. He also looked forward to working with Robert Cary

Gilson, the school's headmaster (principal). Gilson was an outstanding teacher and an inventor. Some boys talked about how he provided electric light for his house by running a small windmill. Others said he had built a machine that copied exam papers.

Gilson pushed his students to ask why and how things happened. It was not enough to memorize facts or learn answers. The *process* of learning was important. Gilson was a master teacher.

Robert Cary Gilson was headmaster at King Edward's between 1900 and 1929.

EARLY FUN WITH WORDS

Ronald's fun with words did not come only from books. His cousins Mary and Marjorie Incledon had created their own language out of animal names. They called it Animalic. Whenever Ronald visited them, he joined in the fun. When Marjorie tired of the language, Mary and Ronald made up a new language. They called it Nivbosh, or New Nonsense. It was light and silly, but the two cousins laughed for hours at their own word inventions.

His students learned to use his approach whether they were trying to understand machines, the law, or the fine arts.

Few students worked harder to learn than Ronald Tolkien. He loved philology, the study of language. He enjoyed learning about grammar, the forms of speech, the sounds of speech, and the meanings of words. He wanted to understand when and why words had first appeared. He was excited to discover the history behind words. He was like a detective looking for clues. One clue led to another until, slowly, answers came.

OLD LANGUAGES

Soon, Ronald met a new challenge through his former instructor George Brewerton, who had remembered Tolkien's interest in Chaucer. He gave his former student an Anglo-Saxon, or Old English, primer (introductory book). The book introduced Ronald to words used by the early English before the 1100s–before the Norman French took over England. For Ronald, the book was a piece of powerful living history. Anglo-Saxon was a strong and forceful language. Ronald also discovered the Old English poem *Beowulf.* Written before 1100, this tale tells of a warrior who fought against two monsters and a dragon. Ronald

This page from *Beowulf* is believed to date to the tenth century. It is the only surviving ancient copy of the text and is kept in the British Museum in London, England.

enjoyed the adventure in both the original Old English form and in modern English.

Following Old English, Ronald continued the trail to Middle English. This was the form of the language in which Chaucer had written *The Canterbury Tales*. *Sir Gawain and the Green Knight* was also written in Middle English. This tale of one of King Arthur's knights, who set out to find a giant, thrilled Ronald.

From Old and Middle English, Ronald moved on to Old Norse. This language comes from the countries of Scandinavia (Denmark, Sweden, and Norway). Old Norse revealed a new collection of word sounds and meanings. Years earlier, Ronald had enjoyed reading a Norse tale called "The Story of Sigurd" in *The Red Fairy Book*. In the tale, Sigurd slays a dragon. Finally, Ronald could read the story in the original Old Norse.

IT'S A FACT!

As a boy, Ronald wanted to have Sigurd's courage and dreamed of slaying dragons himself.

Ronald soon made a new discovery. Cornish's Bookstore, down the road from King Edward's, didn't look like an exciting place from the outside.

But on the dusty shelves inside, Ronald found books written in Greek, Latin, Anglo-Saxon, Old Norse, and German. Each new book offered him a new story and another chance to discover the languages he loved.

Father Morgan encouraged Ronald's interest in languages. He also took his job as guardian to Ronald and Hilary seriously. Each summer, he took them on vacation to Lyme Regis. This seaside town in southwestern England gave Ronald places to roam and sketch, especially on wet mornings when the fog covered the nearby cliffs. Ronald loved to explore the area.

The holidays at Lyme Regis gave the Tolkien boys a chance to tell Father Morgan about how unhappy they were at Aunt Bea's. Father Morgan promised to look for a better place for them in Birmingham.

IT'S A FACT!

On one trip to Lyme Regis, Ronald found a large bone. He thought it was too large to belong to a human. So he decided it must the prehistoric jawbone from a dragon.

CHAPTER

5 SCHOOL DAYS

IN THE SPRING OF 1908, Ronald and Hilary moved to 37 Duchess Road, a boardinghouse run by Mrs. Faulkner. The new home stood peacefully behind the Oratory grounds, near Father Morgan. The new landlady always smiled, a welcome change from Aunt Bea.

But it wasn't Mrs. Faulkner who would have a great influence on the life of sixteen-year-old Ronald Tolkien. It was Edith Bratt, a slender, dark-haired nineteen-year-old girl. She also lived in the Faulkner boardinghouse, below Ronald and Hilary. The more time Ronald Tolkien spent with Edith, the more he liked her. Although she was older, the two seemed to be right for each other.

Like Ronald and Hilary, Edith was an orphan. She was musically talented and played the piano well. She hoped to become a piano teacher or

perhaps to perform in concert halls someday. But for
the time, her guardian had placed her with Mrs.
Faulkner, who was fond of music. The landlady
enjoyed entertaining guests. She liked having Edith
play the piano at her gatherings. But Edith had little
chance to practice on her own. As soon as she
started to practice, Mrs. Faulkner would hurry into
the room and tell her to stop. Mrs. Faulkner wanted
a quiet house when company was not around.

Ronald could have been shy around Edith. After
all, he hadn't known many girls his age. But he wasn't
at all shy. Edith listened to him talk about languages
and the history of words. Her own education was
limited and centered on music. She was eager to learn
more. They laughed about "the old lady," their
nickname for Mrs. Faulkner. They convinced the
maid to sneak snacks for them from the kitchen.

School was more exciting as Ronald
approached his last years at King Edward's. He
studied words and languages more closely. He won
a place in the debating society, where he argued
with his classmates about the issues of the day.
With determination, he defended the goals and
actions of people who supported women's rights. In
other debates, he attacked the character of the

King Edward's School Chronicle.

DEBATING SOCIETY

The first Debate of the Session was held on Friday, October 8th. Mr. Reynolds took the chair, and D.G.J. Macswiney brought forth the motion: "That this house express its sympathy with the objects and its admiration of the tactics of the Militant Suffragette." Women, he said, did not claim universal franchise, but only that sex should be no disqualification in the case of tax-payers. He then drew a pathetic picture of "drunken wretches grovelling in the gutter six nights out of seven," to prove that many men were less worthy of the vote than women. Peaceable methods had been used for forty years without success, and therefore more violent tactics must be used.

A.B. Harrower, who opposed, poured forth the vials of his indignation upon these "Bacchanalian extravagances." To prove his knowledge of the subject, he mentioned that he had bought three Suffragist pamphlets, of which he had read one and lost the others. Woman was naturally a subordinate creature, and the majority did not want the vote.

R.B. Naish did not agree with the Honourable Opener in some points, but was anxious to avoid all appearance of a split on the Affirmative. The question of the vote only became vital in the case of the women of the lower classes, who were unprotected by trades-unionism. C.L. Wiseman pointed out that man had been educated from the middle of the 18th century, but it was not till 1884 that the vote was extended. Woman had had no education till the middle of the 19th century; ergo, they had still fifty years to wait!

F. Scopes argued that the exercise of the vote has an important educative value. He denied the majority of women did not want the vote, and showed that as women were capable of good judgment in municipal affairs, so they would be in those of the nation.

J.R.R. Tolkien (maiden) spoke of the Suffragette from a Zoological point of view and gave an interesting display of his paronomasiac powers. A good humourous speech.

After the Honourable Opener had replied, the House divided, the votes being: Affirmative 12; Negative 20. The motion was therefore lost.

This is part of the November 1909 issue of *King Edward's School Chronicle.* It reports on the debate between J. R. R. Tolkien and his friend Christopher Wiseman.

English writer William Shakespeare. According to *King Edward's School Chronicle,* the school magazine, Ronald also spoke against the historic invasion of England by the Normans of France in 1066. He said the French-speaking Normans had damaged the English language.

Ronald also spent time playing rugby. He was
not big or strong, but he made up for it with
energy and enthusiasm. The *Chronicle* described
Ronald as hard working and determined. The
Chronicle admired his tackling but thought his
kicking skills were quite weak.

Meanwhile, Ronald and Edith had fallen in love.
Hours passed quickly when they were together. This
happy time, though, didn't last. Late in the fall term of
1909, Ronald found himself in trouble. Father Morgan
had learned about the relationship between Ronald

Rugby is similar to football. But in rugby, time-outs, substitutions,
and forward passing are not allowed.

and Edith. The priest was shocked. Father Morgan told Ronald how disappointed he was. In English society at the time, it was improper for Ronald to be seeing a woman who was three years older than he was. He decided that Ronald needed a new place to live and demanded that the relationship end.

Because he had great affection and respect for Father Morgan, Ronald agreed to end the relationship. Instead, he concentrated on his studies. After all, the scholarship exam at Oxford was coming up. Oxford was one of the finest universities in the world. Ronald studied hard to pass the entrance exams and win a scholarship. Without a scholarship, he could not afford to attend the university.

CONCENTRATING ON STUDIES

By the time Ronald took the Oxford test, he felt ready. None of his family had ever gone to a college or university. He wanted to make his family and Father Morgan proud. After the three-day exam was over, Tolkien checked the notice board to learn the results. He had not won an award, but he could try again the following year. Feeling depressed, he walked slowly to the railway station.

The next year, 1910, also began badly. Hilary and Ronald lived in a new boardinghouse. Ronald and Edith tried to stay apart, but eventually they met and took a train ride into the countryside. At a jeweler's shop, they bought and exchanged gifts. Ronald bought Edith a watch for her upcoming twenty-first birthday. She bought a pen for his eighteenth birthday.

Again, Father Morgan learned of their meeting. He told Ronald that there could be no future meetings. They could not even write to each other. Edith's decision to live with an elderly couple in Cheltenham helped the situation. The house was about 50 miles (80 km) away. The distance would make future meetings difficult.

Ronald was not happy with the situation, but he accepted it. Eventually, Father Morgan agreed to let the couple write to each other. But the priest insisted that Ronald direct his attention toward school.

Ronald was in his last year at King Edward's. He took the role of being a member of the first, or senior, class seriously. He prepared a long lecture titled "The Modern Languages of Europe." The first part of the lecture took three hours. The schoolmaster stopped him before he could move on to the second part. His classmates were amazed.

Ronald also continued to play rugby. One game left him with a broken nose, another with a cut tongue. Other boys might have quit, but not Ronald. He loved the sport, and it was worth it to him.

IT'S A FACT!
Ronald had delivered parts of his long lecture in Latin, Greek, and Anglo-Saxon.

FINAL DAYS AT KING EDWARD'S

By December of 1910, Ronald was again headed to Oxford to take the entrance exam. This time, he was confident. On December 17, he learned that he had won a scholarship. It was for 60 pounds ($105) a year, which wasn't much. But combined with money available through King Edward's and with Father Morgan's help, Ronald could afford to go to Oxford University.

His future set, Ronald returned for his final months at King Edward's. His classmates elected him secretary of the debating society. He also became a prefect, or school monitor. With a few other seniors, including Chris Wiseman and the headmaster's son,

Rob Gilson, Ronald helped run the school library. They called their group the Tea Club, or the T.C.

The T.C. members told jokes and drank hot tea in the late afternoon, an old British custom. Ronald enjoyed relaxing with his friends, but he also enjoyed the discussions. When summer came, the Tea Club moved its meetings to the tea room in nearby Barrow's Stores. They changed the name of the club to T.C.B.S. (Tea Club and Barrovian Society). More King Edward's boys, including G. B. Smith, joined the club. They were impressed when Ronald recited from classics such as *Beowulf* and *Sir Gawain and the Green Knight*. Ronald enjoyed the praise and would bow very deeply. This gesture made the other boys laugh. He enjoyed showing his serious side, but he also liked to make people laugh.

In the summer of 1911, the seniors took their final exams at King Edward's. Some were eager to get out. Others feared the idea of being on their own. King Edward's had offered security to Ronald Tolkien. He and his friends had been through a lot together, both good and bad. Soon he would leave it all to begin a new life at Oxford.

CHAPTER 6 SETTING OFF A SPARK

(Above) The library at Oxford's Exeter College was built between 1748 and 1757.

IN THE EARLY 1900s, most of the students attending one of Oxford University's many colleges came from rich families. Ronald's family wasn't rich, and he needed his scholarship and other help to pay his bills. Many of his classmates at Oxford's Exeter College were in similar situations. They had to spend their money carefully. In fact, Exeter College had its beginnings among people who weren't rich.

Ronald arrived at Oxford in a new automobile owned and driven by R. W. Reynolds, one of his former teachers at King Edward's. Reynolds stopped on narrow Turl Street. Ronald saw his name printed on a board at the foot of a staircase. This evidence of belonging made him feel right at home. After climbing the uneven wooden staircase, he reached his new quarters. The place wasn't fancy. It included only a bedroom and a living room. But Ronald thought it was perfect. He was excited to be on his own. All his fears and worries slipped away.

Exeter College offered many activities for new students at Oxford. Ronald signed up for the college essay club and the dialectical society, a formal discussion group. He also played rugby. He started an organization called the Apolausticks. Most of the members were other freshmen. They sat around for hours talking about any topic that a member brought up. Ronald had taken up smoking a pipe. He spruced up his appearance by parting his hair neatly in the center. Tolkien thought of himself as quite an intellectual.

ABOUT OXFORD

Oxford University is Britain's oldest place of higher education. It was founded in the 1100s in the town of Oxford, about 50 miles (80 km) from London, England, the British capital.

Oxford University is made of many colleges, each of which governs itself. Exeter College, where Tolkien went to school, was set up in 1314 by Walter de Stapeldon. Born in southwestern England, he came from a humble background. He later became the bishop of Exeter, a town also in southwestern England, and the treasurer of England.

Stapeldon paid for the founding of the college, which was originally called Stapeldon Hall. He set up the college so that southwestern England would have well-educated religious leaders. Most of the early students—all men—came from this area. By Tolkien's time, though, they came from all over Britain. In 1978, the college started letting in women. In 1993, Exeter became the first of the old all-male colleges to elect a woman as its head.

One evening, the sound of voices drew Ronald and his friends from their rooms. The young men went into the street, where a crowd had formed. Shouts and cheers filled the air. As the crowd grew, no one seemed to care about the cause of it all. Ronald and a friend jumped inside an empty bus that was nearby. Shouting and honking, they drove off. They stopped now and then to pick up other students. Ronald even made speeches to the crowd. Within a few hours, the pranks were over, and all the Oxford students went back to their rooms. No one got into serious trouble, probably because so many people were involved and nothing was damaged.

AN INSPIRATION

Unfortunately, life inside the Exeter classrooms wasn't nearly as exciting for Ronald. He had to force himself to study for some of his classes. Dull instructors presented even duller lectures. However, one instructor, Joseph Wright, sparked Tolkien's imagination.

From age six, Wright had worked in a woolen mill. No

Mill managers liked to hire families with children, since that meant more workers for the mill.

laws at that time protected children against unfair
working conditions. As a child, Wright did not receive
an education. He couldn't read or write. But by the
time he reached his teens, he wanted to learn these
skills. Slowly, he taught himself to read and write.
Then, he taught others. He started going to night
school to study French and German. When he was
twenty-one, he traveled to Germany. At Germany's
University of Heidelberg, he became even more
interested in languages. Whether it was Old English,
Russian, Gothic, or Old Saxon, Wright couldn't get
enough. After he finished school, he returned to
England and took a teaching job at Oxford. He also
started writing dictionaries and language books.

Ronald thought Wright was a fine teacher and
a good role model. Soon, he filled not only a desk
in Wright's classroom but also a place at the Wright
family's dining room table. The eager student ate
and listened to his professor talk about ancient
Greek. Thanks to Wright, Tolkien's spark of interest
in the Welsh language grew. Both men thought it
was a language with beauty in both its sound and
appearance.

During the Christmas holiday of 1911, Tolkien
returned to Birmingham. His old school friends of

the T.C.B.S. were putting on a play called *The Rivals*. They invited him to take part. Tolkien's role was that of Mrs. Malaprop, a woman known for her humorous misuse of words.

During the summer vacation of 1912, Tolkien spent two weeks at a camp with a cavalry group (horse brigade) he had joined. He had fun riding horses over the plains of Kent, a county in the southeastern part of England. But he hated the cold, wet nights. When the camp ended, Tolkien took a vacation in Berkshire, in southern England. He walked the British countryside and sketched the scenes he enjoyed.

When he returned to school, Ronald made a new discovery. A Finnish grammar book opened up a whole new world of language to him. Tolkien studied Finnish poems. He was interested in Finnish gods and goddesses, heroes and villains. The stories held mystery, drama, romance, and adventure. He wondered why such stories had been forgotten. He knew that

IT'S A FACT!

Ronald's discovery of Finnish helped him develop his own unique languages, including Quenya, an Elvish tongue.

the same thing had happened to many of the tales of other cultures. So much had disappeared.

Tolkien thought about creating a British mythology, or set of stories, but he didn't have time. School kept him busy. He had to write papers, essays, and letters home. He even wrote a play for his relatives, with whom he spent Christmas in 1912.

Coming of Age

At midnight on January 3, 1913, Tolkien celebrated his twenty-first birthday. He was finally old enough to marry. He used the occasion to express his love to Edith Bratt in a letter. Edith's reply shocked Ronald. She had doubted his interest in her and had found another boyfriend. She was engaged to a man named George Field.

Sad and confused, Ronald read her letter again and again. Edith had written that she was engaged, but she did not seem happy about it. Not only did Ronald know and understand words, he could also sense the feelings behind them. He boarded a train to Cheltenham, where Edith lived, intending to win her back. She met him at the train station. By the end of the day, she had broken her engagement. When he returned to school, Ronald wrote to Father Morgan about Edith. Although the priest was not pleased, he accepted Ronald's decision.

Ronald turned his attention back to his studies. He had big tests coming up, but he wasn't prepared. He'd been spending too much time with his friends. He quickly wrote papers and reports. They were not his best efforts, and he knew it. When the result came back as "second class," which is like getting a B, he was relieved. He had been lucky to do that well. But he knew he should have been at the first-class level. Because his top score was in philology, Ronald decided to concentrate on that subject. He transferred to the Oxford Honor School of English Language and Literature.

Tolkien knew what he wanted to study. He and Edith talked about marriage. She agreed to become a Catholic and started taking religious instruction. Tolkien felt his long-range plans were shaping up.

It was also important that Ronald finish school and find a job. Schoolwork demanded more attention, since the Oxford Honor School set high standards. There were no shortcuts to success, no quick ways to score high marks. Professors demanded

good writing, and classroom discussions were intense.
With renewed spirit, Tolkien took on his assignments.

In studying one old Anglo-Saxon poem,
Tolkien became intrigued by two lines. He read
them again and again.

Eala Earendel engla beorhtast
ofer middangeard monnum sended.

To most people, the lines meant nothing. But
to Tolkien, the meaning was clear.

Hail Earendel, brightest of angels
above the middle-earth sent unto men.

Tolkien wondered who Earendel was. Whoever
or whatever it was, the lines had a deep effect on
Tolkien. He felt a strange thrill, as if he could grasp
meanings and feelings from the past.

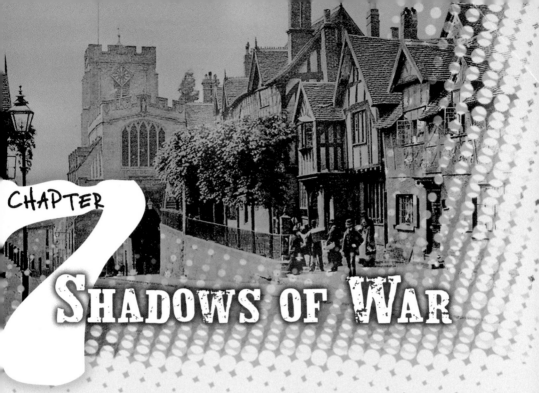

7

SHADOWS OF WAR

LIFE GOT BETTER for Ronald Tolkien early in 1914. On January 8, exactly a year after their reunion, Edith became a Catholic. They soon announced their engagement.

Tolkien fixed up his rooms at Exeter. He bought new furniture and put Japanese prints on his walls. He bought two new suits. The changes gave him a feeling of style and of comfort with himself and his surroundings. The college debating society elected him president. He also captured the Skeat Prize for English, a cash award that Tolkien spent on books.

He often visited Warwick, a city north of Oxford, where Edith was staying with a

(Above) A photo of Warwick, England, where Ronald often went to visit Edith

On his 1914 trip, Tolkien enjoyed the beauty of the seascapes in Cornwall, England.

cousin. The visits gave him an escape from school pressures. He enjoyed the sights and sounds of nature while on long walks. In 1914, he took a trip to Cornwall, a county along the sea in the southwestern part of England. He used the time to sketch and write. He thought about how he would describe the place. He came up with visually clear words. Remembering a line he'd studied earlier about Earendel, Tolkien wrote his own poem about a mythical starship. In the poem, Earendel is the ship's captain. Tolkien called the poem "The Voyage of Earendel the Evening Star." Earendel's night ride continues until dawn's light ends the voyage. Tolkien was pleased with the poem, but he didn't plan to use it again.

IT'S A FACT!

Earendel, the mythical captain, would return in *The Lord of the Rings*. Galadriel gives Frodo a light that shines with the light from Earendel's star.

BECOMING A SOLDIER

While Tolkien's life gained direction and purpose, the outside world grew unstable. By August of 1914, Britain had declared war on Germany. This was the beginning of World War I (1914–1918). Thousands of men in England, Scotland, and Wales signed up to join the British war effort. Hilary Tolkien was one of them. Ronald wanted to finish his studies at Oxford. He was happy to learn that students could get army training while still at school. He signed up, willing to serve his country as soon as he completed his degree.

This was the scene at the Central Recruiting Office in London in August 1914. By September 5, more than 250,000 men had volunteered for service in World War I.

Tolkien enjoyed all the activity. He was busy writing poems and going to classes. He drilled with the training corps. He traveled to see Edith and visited with friends. During this time, he also began to make up another language, influenced by Finnish. By 1915, the new language was taking form. Tolkien spent hours creating poems and stories with the new words.

Tolkien felt confident when he took his final exams. His scores earned him a First, or top honors. He didn't think he'd have much trouble getting a teaching job after his war duties were over.

The new Oxford graduate became a second lieutenant in a British regiment called the Lancashire Fusiliers. His job was to drill, or train, incoming soldiers. Because he looked younger than he was, Tolkien grew a moustache to appear older. On weekends, he jumped on a motorbike and visited Edith in Warwick.

This new life in the army bored Tolkien. He wasn't at Oxford anymore. He fought to stay awake in army lectures and disliked leading boring drills. The food was awful. He found nothing enjoyable about activities focused on how to kill people.

Tolkien was happier when he got the chance to learn signals, the military's form of communication that used codes and not words. Signals were something like new languages. He quickly mastered Morse and other codes. He waved signal flags and shot signal rockets. He spent hours practicing flag signals and light signals.

IT'S A FACT!

Hilary Tolkien joined the 3rd Birmingham Battalion. He was trained as a bugler (someone who plays a hornlike bugle to call troops to order or to signal lights out).

CODES AND SIGNALS

Armies have long communicated in ways that don't use voices or writing. When Tolkien was in the British army, the Morse code and signaling with semaphore flags were both common ways of sending messages.

The Morse code uses short (dit) and long (dah) sounds to stand for letters and numbers. Morse code operators combine the sounds in different ways to send messages. For example, the letters SOS are the short form of the emergency message "save our ship." The letter S is three dits. The letter O is three dahs. In Morse, these letters would come across as "dit-dit-dit, dah-dah-dah, dit-dit-dit."

A signal operator used two semaphore flags, one in each hand. Each position of the flags stood for a letter. This way of communicating had less success because the person to receive the message had to be able to see the operator. This wasn't always likely on the battlefield or at sea.

In any case, being a signal officer during World War I was a lot safer than leading men in warfare. Tolkien may have survived the war because his love for codes and words led him to choose signaling.

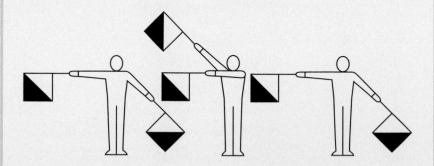

These semaphore flags are sending the message "SOS."

Tolkien knew he would be going to fight in France, but he wasn't sure he would come back. Each day brought more names of soldiers killed in action. Whatever happened, he knew he wanted one dream fulfilled before he sailed. On March 22, 1916, at the age of twenty-four, he married Edith.

Ronald found Edith a place to stay near his army post. She had just settled in when he received orders to leave for France. The newlyweds were sad to part, but they had expected it.

JOINING THE WAR

Early in June 1916, Tolkien headed for London and then on to France. He took some comfort in knowing that his school friends from King Edward's and the T.C.B.S. (Tea Club) were still a part of his life. Chris Wiseman was in the Royal Navy, while Rob Gilson and G. B. Smith were in the British army. They wrote each other, keeping up each other's spirits and remembering good times.

Tolkien found little happiness as he marched across the French countryside. Most marches took place at night, so the enemy couldn't see what was happening. During training drills, the soldiers had used perfect equipment under good

conditions. Field telephones had always been
loud and clear. Men had run along smooth
pathways. Weapons had sparkled in the sunlight.
It had been almost like a game. On the war
front, the phones didn't work, the roads were
blocked or destroyed, and the uniforms were
covered with mud.

And then there were the bodies in trenches
(deep ditches) and on battlefields. Some of the
soldiers were older than Tolkien, but others were

**Most young men thought going off to war would be a great
adventure. But they soon learned how terrible it was. Out
of every 100 soldiers who fought, 63 were killed.**

A British soldier picks at his meal in the trenches. The trench system was important to both sides in protecting soldiers. But life in the trenches was dirty, cold, and miserable.

years younger. Lives that had barely begun were destroyed. Tolkien described trench warfare as an inhuman horror.

The weeks passed as Tolkien's regiment attacked German soldiers in trenches. The soldiers never really knew if they were winning or losing the battle. They rested a little after each attack, but then it all started again.

In July, during the harsh Battle of the Somme, Tolkien received sad news. G. B. Smith wrote that Rob Gilson had been killed. Memories of their happy years at King Edward's came back to Tolkien. Tolkien felt that the T.C.B.S. had ended, but Smith disagreed. In August, Tolkien met Smith, and they talked and ate together.

French soldiers during the Battle of the Somme

THE BATTLE OF THE SOMME

From July to November 1916, French and British troops fought the Germans in the Battle of the Somme *(below)*. This area in northern France was near the Somme River, where the Germans had set up a stronghold. More than 400,000 British men—including G. B. Smith and Rob Gilson, two members of the T.C.B.S.—lost their lives as a result of the battle. The Battle of the Somme is thought to be the bloodiest of World War I.

Poison gas was one of the weapons used in World War I. Soldiers wore gas masks during the Battle of the Somme.

Although Tolkien had managed to escape war injury, in October, he caught a disease the soldiers called "trench fever." He was dizzy and had a high temperature. With treatment, most soldiers recovered in about a week or two, but not Tolkien. His fever wouldn't go away. He was sent back to a hospital in Birmingham, England. Edith hurried to the hospital to look after him.

By mid-December, Tolkien was ready to leave the hospital and go home. But a letter from Christopher Wiseman brought a new sadness and pain. G. B. Smith had died on December 3, 1916.

Again, Tolkien remembered the hopes and dreams of his T.C.B.S. friends. They had planned to do great things. Death had taken Gilson and Smith. Tolkien felt empty and alone.

Tolkien felt something else too. He needed to create. The war had shown him how easily even the young and strong could die. But words and ideas would never die. They could have a lifetime of their own. That thought gave Tolkien a fresh desire to go on.

8

ANSWERING
A CHALLENGE

IN 1917, Ronald Tolkien began putting together the pieces of a puzzle. As he left the military hospital with Edith, Tolkien knew what he wanted to do. He was determined to write a masterpiece, a great story, no matter how long it took.

Perhaps Tolkien wanted to give England a gift. He loved his country, and England did not have its own rich mythology. He remembered reading *The Kalevala,* a collection of Finnish poems that captured the mystery and drama of the people and gods of Finland. He thought that if Finland had a rich collection

**(Above)
Soldiers
wounded in
World War I
recover at a
hospital in
France.**

65

of heroic tales, England should have one too.

Tolkien liked the idea of creating new words, new characters, new places, and new events. In the past, he had created languages just for fun. He had already written poetry, and some of it had even been published. Memories of his years at King Edward's returned, of the T.C.B.S., where his friends had smiled and cheered for some of his poems. Other poems had started serious discussions. Tolkien could never share those moments again with the friends he had lost.

Ronald thought about putting together a long, literary work, but the thought didn't last long. Then he received a note from Chris Wiseman who encouraged him to start writing his epic story. His friend convinced him that he should get to work.

MIDDLE-EARTH IS BORN

Edith brought Ronald from the hospital to Great Haywood, a village not far from his army post. Within days, the recovering soldier began "The Book of Lost Tales." (This work would later become known as *The Silmarillion*.)

Tolkien had read thousands of legends from many countries. He knew how they were set up. But he didn't want to copy any other story. For England, he hoped to write with clear and simple beauty.

For his setting, Tolkien remembered the Norse legend of *Midgard.* In early English, the word meant Middle-earth. Tolkien chose to place the action in an imaginary period long ago. The characters would be elves, dwarves, and evil orcs.

As Tolkien started on his task, Edith helped all she could. She copied his writings in a large book. In the evenings, they relaxed together. He often sketched while she played the piano.

Tolkien's imagination grew with each story. His elves became artists and poets, full of life and energy. Each had a name, a purpose, and a goal. Although they looked like human beings, the characters could not get sick or die, unless they were killed in battle. They had their own language and customs. The task of creating the stories was a challenge Tolkien happily set for himself.

Tolkien wrote every day. He knew that when he was better, he would have to return to his army duties. But just when he seemed to regain his health, his fever would start again. He was in and out of hospitals often during 1917. Edith returned to Cheltenham to stay with a cousin. She was pregnant and needed to take care of herself.

On November 17, 1917, Edith gave birth to a son, John Francis Reuel Tolkien. Soon after, Tolkien felt well enough to return to his military duties. Edith and the baby stayed in the village of Roos, England, near the army base. Tolkien had earned the rank of full lieutenant. This meant he could get leave more often. When they were together, he and Edith often walked in a nearby woods.

Despite his busy schedule, Tolkien continued writing. Most of the stories were about an evil power called Morgoth and the elves of Gondolin. But Tolkien was also inspired by his love for Edith. He expressed his love through the character Beren. Beren falls in love with an elvish maid named Lúthien Tinuviel. To Tolkien, Lúthien represented Edith. The story became the favorite of both Ronald and Edith.

IT'S A FACT!

Tolkien and Edith are buried together in a single grave near Oxford. Its headstone identifies Edith as Lúthien and Tolkien as Beren.

THE WAR ENDS

Edith worked hard to care for the baby, as Tolkien again had to go to the hospital. Edith couldn't hide her jealousy about the amount of bed rest he'd had since his return from France. She probably found the thought of rest very appealing. By the fall of 1918, Tolkien was released from the hospital. He needed to find a job. Surely, he thought, a teaching post was available somewhere.

Tolkien returned to Oxford to seek a job. The university had changed since he had been a student there. Many of the students and teachers who went to war never returned home. As Tolkien walked among the university buildings, he heard the voices of professors lecturing. Visions of old classmates filled his mind. But when he asked about job openings, there were none.

At each stop, the news was bad. Only William Craigie, Tolkien's teacher of the old Icelandic language, offered a small hope. Craigie was working with the staff of *A New English Dictionary on Historical Principles.* Knowing Tolkien's talent for words, Craigie offered him a job working on the project. Tolkien happily accepted.

On November 11, 1918, World War I officially ended. Tolkien wasted no time in contacting his army superiors. He asked to be sent to Oxford to complete his education until he was released from the military service. The army granted his request.

By Christmas, Tolkien was back at Oxford. He lived in rooms near those he had stayed in as a student. But this time, he was with Edith and their baby son. The war was over. He had a job working with words. Tolkien often laughed as he held John Francis in his arms. The future looked bright.

CHAPTER 9

ENTER A HOBBIT

A COLD WIND BLEW as Ronald Tolkien hurried along Broad Street toward the Old Ashmolean Building in Oxford. Once inside, he slipped out of his heavy cloth coat and into a tweed jacket. He lit his pipe and joined the others working on *A New English Dictionary*.

The dictionary had been started in 1858. Some sections had already been published. But the war had caused delays, and the project still needed work. Tolkien was assigned to words beginning with *w*. Many people would have found the work dull, but not Tolkien. He carefully traced the history and meaning of *warm, water,* and *winter.*

A NEW ENGLISH DICTIONARY

When Tolkien started to work on *A New English Dictionary on Historical Principles*, he became part of a huge, long-term project. The idea of the dictionary had come about in 1857, when several British word scholars determined no English language dictionary existed that was either complete or correct. In 1858, these scholars came up with a plan to write a new dictionary.

Each estimate of the time it would take to write the dictionary was way off. By 1884, only one part had been published, and it only covered the words *a* to *ant*! James Murray, the editor at this point, was told to hire more editors and assistants. One of these was William Craigie, who later brought in Tolkien.

Oxford University Press published the full dictionary in 1928 in twenty volumes. Updates to the dictionary—which was officially renamed the *Oxford English Dictionary* in 1933—appeared from time to time. A CD-ROM version first came out in 1992. In 2000, the *Oxford English Dictionary Online* became available for a yearly fee via the Internet.

James Murray was one of the main editors of *A New English Dictionary*.

He wrote each word on a card and sorted them neatly. Each day the stack grew.

Tolkien didn't put in a full day working on the dictionary. He also tutored university students. Most of his students came from the women's colleges of Oxford. Most of these students needed help learning Anglo-Saxon.

By the late summer of 1919, Ronald and Edith could afford to rent a small house. They even hired a cook-housemaid to help Edith, who was pregnant again.

Tolkien was a popular tutor. Students found him patient, and the word spread. Soon he was teaching so much, he could afford to give up his position on the staff of *A New English Dictionary*. When he wasn't tutoring, Tolkien sat at a table and added to "The Book of Lost Tales." At night, he sometimes read to Edith while she played the piano.

Tolkien accepted an invitation to read "The Fall of Gondolin" to some college students. They were fascinated as he shared the battles of heroic elves against the evil Morgoth. At the end, the audience rose, clapping and cheering. Tolkien bowed deeply, grateful for the applause.

PROFESSOR TOLKIEN

During the summer of 1920, Tolkien learned of another job opening. The University of Leeds needed a lecturer and researcher in Anglo-Saxon and Middle English. Leeds was a big industrial city in northern England. The job paid well. With a second child on the way, Tolkien needed the money. He applied for the position and was surprised to get it. Tolkien rode the train northward to Leeds each week and returned to Oxford on weekends. In October, Edith gave birth to a second son, Michael Hilary Reuel Tolkien.

Ronald and Edith didn't like being apart so much. Ever since they had married, Tolkien's war duties and jobs had separated them. Late in 1921, they rented a small house in Leeds. At least their family was together.

In 1922, Eric Gordon joined the English staff at Leeds. Gordon had known Tolkien while both were at Oxford. In fact, Tolkien had tutored Gordon in 1919. They began working together on a new modern English edition of the Middle English poem *Sir Gawain and the Green Knight*. Their new edition included notes on the poem and its

The Great
Hall at the
University
of Leeds

meaning, as well as a glossary. Students and
teachers alike praised their work.

Tolkien did not only write books for school
use. He also wrote more myths and legends. Some
of his writing appeared in magazines. "The Book of
Lost Tales" kept growing. He created a universe for
his story. He then wrote a tale about Feanor, a
craftsman. Feanor created the Silmarils, the
beautiful yet deadly jewels stolen by the evil
Morgoth. But each time Tolkien came close to

completing the story, he stopped to change parts of it. He wanted it to be perfect.

In 1924, at age thirty-two, Tolkien was promoted to a full professor at the University of Leeds. Few teachers achieved such a high position so young. Ronald and Edith celebrated by buying a house on the outskirts of the city. Open fields where the children could play surrounded the brick house. The timing was perfect. In November, a third son, Christopher Reuel Tolkien, was born.

As happy as he was at Leeds, Tolkien wished he could return to Oxford. In late winter of 1925, he learned there was an opening there. He quickly applied, but three other fine candidates applied for the job too. Tolkien held out little hope for getting it. When he learned that he had been accepted for the position of professor of Anglo-Saxon, he almost dropped the pipe he had been smoking.

In 1926, the family moved into a pale brick house on Northmoor Road in North Oxford. It had high ceilings, and ivy

IT'S A FACT!

Although Tolkien attended Exeter College, he ended up teaching at Merton College. This is another college in the Oxford system.

The Tolkiens lived in this house on Northmoor Road.

plants covered the outside. The Tolkiens remained on Northmoor Road for more than twenty years. From there, Ronald bicycled to his classes.

Tolkien received a warm welcome from the other teachers at Oxford. Another professor and writer named C. S. Lewis became a close friend. Together they started clubs where they could read their work aloud. One such club was the Inklings. Tolkien welcomed the chance to get to know others with interests in language and literature.

C. S. Lewis

Clive Staples Lewis *(right),* Tolkien's Oxford friend and fellow Inkling, wrote science fiction, religious works, and children's stories. *Out of the Silent Planet* is a story about scientists on Mars. In *The Screwtape Letters,* an old devil gives funny advice to a young devil.

Lewis is perhaps best known for the *Chronicles of Narnia,* a seven-book series for children that combines myths and fantasy. The stories mostly involve the four Pevensie children—Lucy, Susan, Edmund, and Peter. They go through a magic cupboard and enter Narnia. This magical world has friendly dwarves, hungry giants, evil dragons, and many talking animals. The children help the inhabitants of Narnia get out of trouble again and again. Lewis's works are considered classic children's tales.

But Tolkien's favorite audience was at home. He told his eldest son, John, about the adventures of a red-headed boy called Carrots, who climbed into a cuckoo clock. As soon as they were old enough, Michael and Chris begged for stories too. The boys enjoyed their father's stories of elves and dwarves. They liked to see the sketches he made of the characters. They also enjoyed hearing about dragons and orcs, even if the stories scared them. Always, Ronald's sons begged to hear more.

In 1929, Edith Tolkien gave birth to a daughter, Priscilla Mary Reuel. At last, after having three boys, Edith had the daughter she had hoped for.

BILBO BAGGINS

For Ronald Tolkien, another birth took place that year. He was at home one afternoon grading exam papers. He wore his usual gray tweed jacket and was puffing on his pipe. As he worked, he noticed that a student had left a page blank. He thought that, after so many pages filled with words, the blank page appeared very empty and alone. He felt like he almost had to write on it. Then a sentence popped into his head: "In a hole in the ground there lived a hobbit."

A "hobbit?" What exactly was a hobbit? In all the languages he had studied, Tolkien had never

IT'S A FACT!

Every year, Tolkien wrote his children illustrated letters from Father Christmas. This is the British name for Santa Claus. These letters were published in 1976 as *Letters from Father Christmas.*

seen the word *hobbit.* He sat back and smiled. The word interested him. He wanted to learn more about his hobbit.

Before long, Tolkien had named his hobbit Bilbo Baggins. Much like Tolkien himself, Bilbo was middle-aged, smoked a pipe, and had few worries. Tolkien soon decided that he could not have only one hobbit. There had to be more. He imagined the hobbits as being much like English people of years ago, just smaller in size. They lacked imagination but had plenty of courage.

Tolkien tried out his hobbit tales on his children. Each night, they listened as Bilbo searched for treasure through woods and tunnels. He faced mean trolls, angry dragons, and other dangers. The boys liked the stories and wanted their father to tell them more. Tolkien wrote down the adventures he made up during these storytelling sessions. He thought perhaps they would be published someday.

The Inklings liked the hobbit tales too. Sometimes his stories rhymed, sometimes they didn't, but Tolkien always tried to keep his reader or listener wanting to know what would happen next. He also liked making the reader do some of

This sign hangs on a wall in a pub (bar and restaurant) that was one of the Inklings' favorite spots.

C. S. LEWIS,
his brother, W. H. Lewis, J. R. R. Tolkien,
Charles Williams and other friends
met every Tuesday morning, between
the years 1939-1962 in the back room
of this their favourite pub. These men,
popularly known as the "Inklings," met
here to drink Beer and to discuss,
among other things, the books they
were writing.

the work. He didn't try to make every point clear. Through Bilbo, Tolkien wanted to give readers a chance to create adventures. Tolkien gave them the general ideas, but he wanted his readers to use their own imaginations.

Tolkien's work on *The Hobbit* went well until it was about three-quarters done. The dragon Smaug had just been killed. But then Tolkien stopped writing. The boys had outgrown Tolkien's nighttime story sessions, and he had set the story aside. Lewis and other Inkling members kept asking for more adventures, but Tolkien had started thinking about other things.

Nevertheless, word of the story got out. Elaine Griffiths, one of Tolkien's former students, had gone to work for a London publisher, George Allen & Unwin Ltd. She told people at the publishing company about the adventures of Bilbo Baggins. One day in 1936, an editor knocked at Tolkien's door. By the end of their visit, the editor carried the story back to London to publish it.

Soon, Tolkien got a letter from Allen & Unwin. The editors liked the story, but they wondered about the ending. Their interest in the story got Tolkien started again. By October of 1936, he had finished it.

WIN SOME, LOSE SOME

Tolkien had to give up some of his ideas about the design of *The Lord of the Rings*. The publishers could not afford to pay for the special treatment that would make the pages of one section look old and burned. The printers wanted to change the spelling of certain words, but Tolkien insisted on using his own spelling. He preferred *elven* to *elfin, elvish* to *elfish,* and *dwarves to dwarfs.* The publishers also had problems with Tolkien's maps. Christopher Tolkien, a writer and artist, stepped in to help with those.

The final decision to publish the book rested with ten-year-old Rayner Unwin, the son of the publishing company's chairman. When the boy wrote about how much he liked the story, the decision was made. *The Hobbit* was scheduled for publication.

Tolkien worried about how the book would look and be received. The publishers decided the book needed illustrations. They asked to see the drawings Tolkien had done for the story. They accepted eight of the ten illustrations he sent them. Next, Tolkien had to redo many of the maps for the book. He then chose to rewrite parts of the story. It never seemed to be just right. Finally, he had to let it be printed.

The first copy *The Hobbit,* also called *There and Back Again,* appeared on September 21, 1937. A nervous J. R. R. Tolkien flipped through the pages of the volume, wondering what people would think of his story.

CHAPTER 10
BILBO TRIUMPHS

(Above)
Tolkien was forty-five years old when *The Hobbit* was published. The book was very popular, and he soon became famous.

NEWSPAPER REVIEWS of *The Hobbit* came in quickly. Tolkien's friend C. S. Lewis wrote the review in the *Times* of London. He wrote: "All who love that kind of children's book which can be read and re-read by adults should take note that a new star has appeared. . . ."

Others praised the story as well. Allen & Unwin compared *The Hobbit* to Lewis Carroll's *Alice in Wonderland,* since both authors were Oxford teachers. But some reviewers saw important differences between the two stories. One reviewer suggested that while Carroll had introduced a cast of fascinating characters, Tolkien gave readers a journey into a completely new world. Another reviewer wrote that opening Tolkien's book was like opening a chest filled with treasure that sparkled and amazed.

Tolkien was very happy with the response. He was also glad to learn that he would earn some extra money from the book. With four children, Tolkien needed all the money he could get.

By Christmas of 1937, the first edition of *The Hobbit* had sold out in England. When *The Hobbit* was published in the United States a year later, it again received outstanding reviews. "This is one of the most freshly original and delightfully imaginative books for children that have appeared in many a long day.... *The Hobbit* is a glorious account of a magnificent adventure, filled with suspense and seasoned with a quiet humor that is irresistable," wrote one newspaper reviewer. The reviewer went on to say, "Here, too, are set down clearly the distinguishing characteristics of dwarves, goblins, trolls and elves. The account of the journey is so explicit that we can readily follow the progress of the expedition. . . . Boys and girls from 8 years on have already given *The Hobbit* an enthusiastic welcome, but this is a book with no age limits. All those, young or old, who love a fine adventurous tale, beautifully told, will take *The Hobbit* to their hearts."

A SEQUEL

Tolkien had little time to enjoy the praise. Already Stanley Unwin, one of his British publishers, was asking for a sequel, or a follow-up, to *The Hobbit*.

Stanley Unwin

Tolkien wondered if this might be the time to publish the giant collection of myths, legends, and songs he had begun so long ago. Once called "The Book of Lost Tales," he renamed it *The Silmarillion.* The title came from the three great jewels that were so important to the story. Tolkien sent the story to his publishers. He also sent them several short stories for children.

His publishers were not interested in these stories. They wanted another hobbit book. Readers everywhere seemed to want the same thing–more hobbits. Tolkien agreed to try.

Tolkien tried to introduce a new hobbit, Bilbo's son Bingo Baggins. But that character didn't interest him. Instead, Tolkien created Bilbo's nephew, Bingo Bolger Baggins, who would find a ring. The ring would be a connection to *The Hobbit.* Tolkien quickly began work on the story. (Later, he would change the new hobbit's name to Frodo.)

Once the story took form, Tolkien sent it to his publishers. He asked that Rayner Unwin again look it over. After all, the boy had been most helpful with the first story.

As Tolkien continued to work on the book, he felt the story changing. It drifted away from the

Elijah Wood *(left)* played the hobbit Frodo in *The Lord of the Rings* films. Here, he holds up a huge version of the ring that is the focus of the story.

light, happy style of *The Hobbit*. The language was more adult, and the thoughts were deeper. Tolkien couldn't check in with his audience either. All his children were grown now, beyond storytelling age. Years passed. Tolkien tried again and again to force the story. He just was never happy with it.

Outside events distracted him as well. His son Christopher developed a heart problem. He had to stay in bed and needed constant attention. Tolkien and his wife took turns watching over their son. Christopher slowly regained his strength.

Britain's entry into World War II (1939–1945) changed the student population at Oxford. Many of Oxford's young men were entering the army. They took "short courses" before becoming officers. Tolkien taught many of these students, making courses and lectures shorter. Tolkien also volunteered to be an air-raid warden. He would help warn the town if enemy planes were coming. But Oxford was never directly attacked.

Despite the distractions, Tolkien continued to work on his sequel to *The Hobbit*. He called it *The Lord of the Rings*. By the end of 1942, he sent word to Stanley Unwin that it was almost finished.

But by the middle of 1943, Tolkien told his

IT'S A FACT!

Tolkien's Black Riders remind some readers of Germany's Nazi Black Corps, or SS. These Nazi troops dressed in black uniforms and terrorized people throughout Europe during World War II. They were to obey Germany's leader, Adolf Hitler, their Nazi leader, without question, just as the Black Riders were to obey Sauron.

Tolkien in his office at Merton College

publisher that he was stuck again. No matter how hard he tried, Tolkien couldn't seem to finish the story. He worked long into the night. Although he hated waking up early, he did so to continue his work. He wanted a map to record the action. The names of the characters had to be perfect. The words had to be just right.

Christopher Tolkien tried to help. Christopher also loved writing, and he was training to be a pilot. His father mailed him letters describing the book's progress. Christopher sent back his ideas. Tolkien's friend C. S. Lewis and another Inkling, Charles Williams, also helped to get the book finished.

Tolkien appreciated the help. But he knew that it was up to him to get the job done. Progress on *The Lord of the Rings* was slow. In 1949, Allen & Unwin published a funny Tolkien story about heroes and dragons called *Farmer Giles of Ham.* It was published in the United States the following year. For years, Tolkien fans had been told another hobbit book was coming. With the appearance of *Farmer Giles of Ham,* more people asked about the new hobbit book.

Tolkien's readers remained excited about the new book, but to Tolkien himself, the job of writing it was tiring. Finally, he decided that he had to finish it. In February 1950, after twelve years of work, he wrote to Allen & Unwin to announce that *The Lord of the Rings* was done.

SUNSET OVER MIDDLE-EARTH

Tolkien's publishers were happy to learn that *The Lord of the Rings* was finally finished. But they still were not interested in publishing *The Silmarillion,* which Tolkien wanted to see in print. *The Silmarillion* was important to Tolkien. It was a memorial to the former schoolmates who were killed in World War I. To Tolkien, it was a matter of honor to see it published. But Allen & Unwin disagreed.

Tolkien decided to find a new publishing house to publish both books. Collins Publishing showed immediate interest. The only problem was that *The Lord of the Rings* was almost half a million words long. In postwar Britain, paper was scarce. Collins wanted Tolkien to make the story shorter. Tolkien felt it had already been cut as much as possible. He also wanted to do some final work on *The Silmarillion*. He thought it would end up being half a million words too. Because of paper costs, Collins Publishing backed away from the deal. Tolkien took his work back to Allen & Unwin. He agreed to Allen & Unwin's idea of publishing only *The Lord of the Rings*. The publisher was glad to have him back again.

While Tolkien was struggling with his publishing problems, he and Edith were trying to find a new home. As the boys grew up and left home, the house on Northmoor Road seemed too

The Tolkien home on Sandfield Road in Headington

large for their needs. In 1950, Ronald, Edith, and Priscilla moved into a house on Holywell Street, but the traffic there was too noisy. In the spring of 1953, the Tolkiens moved into a house in Headington, just east of Oxford.

Publishing *The Lord of the Rings* continued to be a battle. Allen & Unwin could not publish the work as one book. It had to be released as a trilogy, or in three separate volumes. Tolkien insisted that *The Lord of the Rings* remain as the overall title. The three individual books would be called *The Fellowship of the Ring, The Two Towers,* and *The Return of the King.*

In August 1954, *The Fellowship of the Ring* was released. The book got good reviews in the United States as well as in Britain. Tolkien was pleased that most of the reviews were good.

Tolkien promised to supply an index of names for *The Lord of Rings* series. But as he worked on it, the demand for the other two volumes increased. They were published without Tolkien's index. Soon publishers in foreign countries got the publishing rights to translate the books into other languages. J. R. R. Tolkien became a literary name known all over the world.

Invitations to speak poured in. Each day brought letters from

IT'S A FACT!

As a result of the popularity of *The Lord of the Rings,* Tolkien had to get an unlisted telephone number. He and his wife could no longer bear the crowds gawking at their house and the middle-of-the-night phone calls from strangers.

readers praising his work, and gifts came too. The author was pleased people enjoyed his work, but he felt the stories, not the author, were important. He said that all he ever wanted to do was entertain his readers.

NEW CHALLENGES

In the summer of 1959, Tolkien gave his final lecture at Oxford, at the age of sixty-seven. He knew it would not be easy to give up the work he had been doing for forty years. But time was catching up with him. His steps had slowed. Sometimes his speech was hard to understand. Wrinkles lined his face, and the days of bicycling to classes were behind him.

Edith had also aged. Her joints hurt because of arthritis. The couple moved often in search of a home that required less upkeep. The peaceful seaside town of Bournemouth held a special charm for her. Although Tolkien hated to leave the Oxford community, he knew Edith preferred Bournemouth. In 1968, they made the move.

Through the years, Tolkien continued to work on *The Silmarillion.* Allen & Unwin finally wanted to publish it. After all, *The Lord of the Rings* trilogy

Edith enjoyed life in Bournemouth, England *(above, pictured from the sea)*.

had sold millions of copies. In the United States, the books had a special following among college students. The books were on reading lists and were talked about in college classes. One professor in the United States wrote that his student rated Tolkien among England's three greatest authors, along with William Shakespeare and Charles Dickens.

Every once in awhile, another Tolkien title appeared, though none matched the popularity of the hobbit books. Still, *The Silmarillion* waited to be finished.

In 1971, at the age of seventy-nine, Tolkien decided to complete the book, which he had begun in 1917. At his empty desk, he sat puffing on his pipe and studying notebooks and boxes full of papers. He looked carefully over all his notes. He reviewed the chapters he had written and rewritten so often.

Then something happened to delay his work. In the middle of November, Edith became ill. She went to the hospital because of gallbladder problems. On Monday, November 29, 1971, she died at the age of eighty-two. Tolkien had lost his loving companion after fifty-five years of marriage.

IT'S A FACT!

Musical groups got into Tolkien's works in the 1960s and 1970s. Led Zeppelin borrowed themes for the song "Ramble On." And The Beatles wanted to star in a *Lord of the Rings* movie. John Lennon would be Gollum. George Harrison would play Gandalf. Paul McCartney saw himself as Frodo. And Ringo Starr would be Sam. However, Tolkien disliked the idea, and the project died.

After Edith died, Tolkien returned to Oxford to live at 21 Merton Street.

By March 1972, Tolkien had moved back to Oxford. His son John was a Catholic priest. Michael and Christopher had followed their father's footsteps into the classroom as teachers. Priscilla was working as a probation officer. All the children came often to visit their father.

The world also remembered the author. In the spring of 1972, Tolkien visited Buckingham Palace for a visit with Queen Elizabeth II. She made him a Commander of the Order of the British Empire. This award recognized his literary efforts. On June 4, he returned to Oxford to receive an Honorary Doctorate of Letters for his work in philology. The following June, he was off to Edinburgh, Scotland, for another honorary degree. Many more invitations had to be declined.

As the weeks passed, Tolkien's steps became slower. He seemed to tire more quickly. In late August 1973, Tolkien traveled to Bournemouth to visit friends. He complained of stomach cramps and went to a hospital. Doctors discovered that he had a bleeding ulcer and quickly called the family. Michael and Christopher were out of the country, but John and Priscilla hurried to be with their father. After a brief recovery, Tolkien developed a chest infection. He died on Sunday, September 2, 1973, at the age of eighty-one.

IT'S A FACT!

As a Commander of the Order of the British Empire, Tolkien could be called Sir John Ronald Reuel Tolkien. His wife would've been called Lady Tolkien.

The gravestone of Edith and J. R. R. Tolkien recalls the story of Beren and Lúthien, which Tolkien wrote in 1917.

News of Tolkien's death saddened people around the world. Four days later, Father John Tolkien presided at the funeral Mass for his father in Oxford. Family and friends gathered to pray for the man who had enriched their lives.

Four years later, in 1977, Christopher Tolkien guided to publication the volume his father had begun sixty years earlier. *The Silmarillion* quickly found its place among the other works created by the man whom some called the Master of Fantasy.

"FRODO LIVES"

The popularity of *The Hobbit* and *The Lord of the Rings* trilogy stayed strong, even after Tolkien's death. In the 1990s, reports said that more than forty million copies of the books were in print. And the books had been translated into as many as forty languages.

But numbers are only one measure of Tolkien's popularity. The word *hobbit* entered the *Oxford English Dictionary*. When Tolkien was working on *A New English Dictionary* so long ago, he probably never thought that he would make his own contribution to such a collection of words.

IT'S A FACT!

Director George Lucas has said *The Lord of the Rings* trilogy was a major influence for his 1980s *Star Wars* movies.

In the mid-1990s, New Line Cinema announced plans to create film versions of *The Lord of the Rings*. In 2001, *The Fellowship of the Ring,* the first of these movies, was finally released. The film was an instant hit and won four Academy Awards. The release of the film also started a new wave of Tolkien-mania. Tolkien websites, *Lord of the Rings* action figures, and increased *Lord of the Rings* book sales worldwide are just a few examples of Tolkien's renewed popularity.

IT'S A FACT!

Actor Christopher Lee, who played Saruman in the LOTR movie trilogy, once met Professor Tolkien in an English pub. Ian McKellen, the actor who played Gandalf, has said that he based his portrayal of Gandalf on Tolkien himself.

Fans eagerly lined up for the first midnight showings of *The Two Towers* (2002) and *The Return of the King* (2003). Both movies were wildly successful on screen and as DVDs.

The Return of the King was the second movie ever to make more than one billion dollars worldwide at the box office. (The other movie was 1997's *The Titanic*.) And in 2004, *The Return of the King* made a clean sweep at the Oscars, winning all eleven of the awards for which it was nominated. The two major awards were for Best Picture and Best Director. But the film was also honored for its music, makeup, and costuming.

The writers, who based their work on Tolkien's books, each got an Oscar. Each major member of the team that created the special effects was honored.

It seems that Tolkien's place in literary history remains secure every place on earth and in Middle-earth as well. As so many people have proclaimed, "Frodo lives."

IT'S A FACT!

In January 2003, fans all over the world celebrated Tolkien's 111th—or as the hobbits would have called it, his eleventy-first—birthday.

Anglican Church: the organization that oversees the main form of Christianity that is followed in England. In Tolkien's time, people in England who didn't follow this faith were looked down upon.

boardinghouse: a place where people pay money to live and receive meals

Britain: the country in northern Europe that is made up of England, Scotland, Wales, and Northern Ireland

British Empire: the huge, historic holdings of the nation of Britain, including its many colonies and territories around the world. South Africa, where Arthur Tolkien worked, was part of this empire until 1961.

Catholic Church: the organization that oversees a major form of Christianity. England rejected the Catholic form in the 1500s and replaced it with the Anglican form. In Tolkien's time, people in England who followed the Catholic faith were looked down upon.

grammar book: a book that talks about the rules for speaking and writing a language

Greek: the language spoken by Greeks. Tolkien studied ancient Greek. Few people write or speak ancient Greek, but modern students read works in the old language.

Inklings: a group of men who met weekly to discuss their literary works in progress. The group's name came from the definition of inkling–an idea that is not completely formed.

Lancashire Fusiliers: a regiment of the British army that has ties to the historic county of Lancashire. A fusilier was once a person who shot a type of light firearm called a fusil or musket. By Tolkien's time, rifles had replaced fusils.

Latin: the language spoken by the ancient Romans. By Tolkien's time, it had become a language that wasn't used much, either in written or spoken form.

Methodist Church: another form of Christianity that came from a movement for reform within the Anglican Church. By the late 1700s, the Methodist Church was independent of the Anglican Church.

mythology: a collection of myths, or stories, about gods or goddesses that describe a culture's way of viewing life, nature, and human relationships

role model: a person whose good behavior is copied by others

trench fever: a disease marked by fever and pain in the muscles, bones, and joints

trench warfare: a style of fighting in which opposing forces attack and counterattack from long, narrow trenches dug into the earth and protected by barbed wire

tutor: to give private lessons to one student at a time

women's rights: legal, political, and social rights for women equal in every area to the rights of men

World War I: a global conflict fought between Germany and its allies and Britain, the United States, and their allies from 1914 to 1918 in Europe and the Middle East.

A Tolkien Literary Glossary

Bilbo Baggins: a hobbit who helps the dwarves reclaim their stolen treasure in *The Hobbit.* He reappears in the trilogy.

Frodo Baggins: Bilbo's heir and one of the main characters of the trilogy. His efforts eventually destroy the One Ring.

dwarf: a short, stocky creature, who tends to prefer the company only of other dwarves

elf: the oldest creature in Middle-earth. Elves are sensitive, with great powers of sight and hearing.

Gandalf: a powerful wizard who alone knows the entire history of Sauron and the One Ring

Gollum: formerly a hobbit, a creature who comes under the power of Sauron and the One Ring

hobbit: a short creature with furry feet who lives in the Shire

Middle-earth: the setting for Tolkien's trilogy. Tolkien insisted that Middle-earth was simply Earth at an earlier time, when life on our planet was different.

Old Forest: a small forested area near the hobbits' Shire. They cross it to escape the Black Riders in *The Fellowship.*

One Ring: a ring forged by Sauron, who gives it great evil power

orc: an evil creature who looks like a goblin

Quenya: one of two elvish languages created by Tolkien. He developed its written form and its grammar.

Saruman: a wizard who eventually comes under the power of Sauron

Sauron: a mighty evil spirit, who gives the One Ring its power

Shelob: a man-eating creature in the shape of a massive spider

Smaug: a greedy dragon in *The Hobbit* who steals the dwarves' treasure

Weathertop: a major hill between the hobbits' Shire and Rivendell, a safe area controlled by elves

SOURCE NOTES

5 "'Rings' Team a Shining Inspiration," *New Zealand Herald*, February 3, 2004, <http://www.nzherald.co.nz/storydisplay.cfm?storyID=3552243&thesection=news&thesubsection=general&thesecondsubsection=reportid=56531> (June 25, 2004).

6 J. R. R. Tolkien, interview with Dennis Gerrolt, *Now Read On*, BBC Radio 4, January 1971. Transcript found online at <http://www.newsfrombree.co.uk> (June 25, 2004).

84 Humphrey Carpenter, *J. R. R. Tolkien: A Biography* (London: Allen & Unwin, 1977), 182.

85–86 Anne T. Eaton, "A Delightfully Imaginative Journey," *New York Times*, March 13, 1938, <http://www.nytimes.com/1938/03/13/movies/LORT-HOBBIT.html> (June 23, 2004).

SELECTED BIBLIOGRAPHY

Bingham, Jane M., ed. *Writers for Children.* New York: Charles Scribner's Sons, 1988.

Carpenter, Humphrey. *J. R. R. Tolkien: A Biography.* London: Allen & Unwin, 1977; Boston: Houghton Mifflin Co., 1977.

Commire, Anne, ed. *Something about the Author.* Vol. 32. Detroit: Gale Research, 1983.

Giddings, Robert, ed. *J. R. R. Tolkien: This Far Land.* New York: Barnes and Noble, 1984.

Helms, Randel. *Tolkien's World.* Boston: Houghton Mifflin Co., 1975.

Kocher, Paul. *Master of Middle-earth: The Achievement of J. R. R. Tolkien.* Boston: Twayne Publishers, 1980.

Tyler, J. E. A., ed. *The New Tolkien Companion.* New York: St. Martin's Press, 1979.

FURTHER READING AND WEBSITES

BBC Schools Online: World War One.
<http://www.bbc.co.uk/schools/worldwarone/>
Learn about World War I by looking at the belongings of soldiers and civilians.

Campbell, Janis, and Cathy Collison. *Authors by Request: An Inside Look at Your Favorite Writers.* Hillsboro, OR: Beyond Words Publishing, Inc., 2002.

Coren, Michael. *J. R. R. Tolkien: The Man Who Created the Lord of the Rings.* New York: Scholastic, 2001.

Cox, Brenda S. *Who Talks Funny? A Book about Languages for Kids.* North Haven, CT: Linnet Books, 1995.

Feldman, Ruth Tenzer. *World War I.* Minneapolis: Lerner Publications Company, 2004.

Levine, Stuart P. *The Importance of J. R. R. Tolkien*. San Diego: Lucent Books, 2003.

Official Lord of the Rings Movie Site.
<http://www.lordoftherings.net/>
Information about New Line Cinema's movies straight from the source.

TheOneRing.net.
<http://www.theonering.net>
This is a large site for fans of *The Lord of the Rings*.

Serkis, Andy. *Gollum: How We Made Movie Magic*. Boston, MA: Houghton Mifflin, 2003.

Sibley, Brian. *The Lord of the Rings Official Movie Guide*. Boston: Houghton Mifflin, 2001.

Tolkien in Oxford.
<http://www.jrrtolkien.org.uk/>
This is a very broad website covering all aspects of Tolkien's life.

SELECTED WORKS BY TOLKIEN

The Adventures of Tom Bombadil and Other Verses from the Red Book. London: Unwin Hyman, 1990.

Farmer Giles of Ham. Boston: Houghton Mifflin Co., 1999.

The Fellowship of the Ring: Being the First Part of The Lord of the Rings. Boston: Houghton Mifflin Co., 2003.

The Hobbit, or There and Back Again. Boston: Houghton Mifflin Co., 2001.

Letters from Father Christmas. Edited by Baillie Tolkien. Boston: Houghton Mifflin Co., 1999.

Letters of J. R. R. Tolkien: a Selection. Edited by Humphrey Carpenter, with the assistance of Christopher Tolkien. Boston: Houghton Mifflin Co., 2000.

The Return of the King: Being the Third Part of The Lord of the Rings. Boston: Houghton Mifflin Co., 2003.

The Silmarillion. Edited by Christopher Tolkien. Boston: Houghton Mifflin Co., 2001.

The Tolkien Reader. New York: Del Ray, 1989.

The Two Towers: Being the Second Part of The Lord of the Rings. Boston: Houghton Mifflin Co., 2003.

Unfinished Tales of Númenor and Middle-earth. Edited by Christopher Tolkien. Boston: Houghton Mifflin Co., 2001.

INDEX

ACKNOWLEDGMENTS

Photographs are used with the permission of: © AP/Wide World, pp. 4, 77; © Hulton-Deutsch Collection/CORBIS, pp. 11, 39, 63; SATOUR, p. 12; © Bettmann/CORBIS, pp. 15, 23, 78; Library of Congress, p. 17; King Edward's School, Birmingham, pp. 19, 31, 38; © Historical Picture Archive/CORBIS, p. 25; © Hulton|Archive by Getty Images, pp. 33, 72, 90; © Brian Harding; Eye Ubiquitous/ CORBIS, p. 44; North Carolina State Archives, p. 47; © Mansell Collection/Time & Life Pictures/Getty Images, pp. 53, 54, 56; Laura Westlund, p. 58; © Underwood & Underwood/CORBIS, p. 61; Illustrated London News, p. 62; Trustees of the Imperial War Museum, pp. 60, 65; University of Leeds, p. 75; David Dettman, pp. 81 (left), 93, 98, 100; Linda Watt, p. 81 (right); © Time Life Pictures/Getty Images, p. 84; © Getty Images, pp. 86, 88; © Sean Sexton Collection/CORBIS, p. 96.

Cover: © Bettmann/CORBIS.